Kemi Itayemi

FROM WOUNDS TO WHOLENESS

BRINGING HEALING TO
THOSE WHO FEEL
WORTHLESS, IMPRISONED,
AND ISOLATED

Copyright © 2023 Kemi Itayemi

Published by Krystal Lee Enterprises LLC (KLE Publishing)
All rights reserved. No parts of this book may be reproduced, distributed, or used in any manner, including photocopying, recording, or other electronic or mechanical methods without the prior written permission of the copywriter owner, except for the use of brief quotations in a book review and certain noncommercial uses permitted by copyright law.

Paperback: 978-1-945066-29-0
All rights reserved. Please send comments and questions:
Krystal Lee Enterprises
sales@KLEPub.com

To Reach the Author:
Email: info@kemispeaks.com
Web: Kemispeaks.com / Media: @Kemispeaksofficial
FB Group: Leaping GIANTS   Contact: Phone: (703) 719-8399
Fax: (703) 988-7860

Printed in the United States of America.
Disclaimers
The information in this book was correct at the time of publication, but the Author does not assume any liability for loss or damage caused by errors or omissions. These are my memories, from my perspective, and I have tried to represent events as faithfully as possible.

Dedication

To my children,
The greatest treasures of my life. You have been with me on every step of my journey, through the ups and downs, and the twists and turns.

You have challenged me to become a better person and have given me the strength to face any obstacle that comes my way.

As you read this book, I hope it brings you inspiration and wisdom. May it remind you of the love that surrounds you and the endless possibilities that await you.
Thank you for being my constant companions on this journey called life. I love you more than words can express.

Contents

Preface 7

Introduction 11

Chapter 1
    The Burden of Being Different 17

Chapter 2
    How Childhood Experiences Manifest In
    Adult Relationships................................ 29

Chapter 3
    Befriending Fear 45

Chapter 4
    Know Youself... 55

Chapter 5
    Welcoming the Divine 65

Chapter 6
    Practicing Detachment......................... 73

Chapter 7
    Living Your Best Life............................ 81

Let's Connect 89

About the Author 91

KLE Publishing 93

Preface

Have you noticed how music, a sound, noise, or words can transport you back in time? A song can bring a warming nostalgia or it can recreate a deep hidden truth that you had hoped time would allow you to forget. Many of us don't have perfect childhoods, sure, but some of us grew up under peculiar circumstances.

I didn't realize how much my childhood experiences shaped my adulthood until I ended up in counseling. I am a firm believer that every human being needs some type of coaching /counseling during the course of our lives. When we are on the go, it is easy to be busy living life and forget to analyze in what direction our life is going. No one wakes up one day inside a bad marriage, raising children that do not respect them, or having a job that ignores their gifts and talents. This world was crafted by our mindset, attitude, expectations, and boundaries or the lack thereof.

It is a humbling experience to see that your life is in trouble and the number one person responsible is you. No, you are not to blame for why people have treated you the way they have, but you determine what you accept. We cannot erase our past but we can choose to get healing from our past.

This journey of healing can be scary when you are alone. I remember going to counseling and the fear that gripped me as I spoke the words of confirmation from my mouth. When I could see the error in my own thoughts, within my own heart, I knew I had to make a sharp change. It was not easy to make this life transition and I desperately wanted to have someone walk this journey with me.

Yes counseling started me on my way and helped me do some heavy lifting, but the work is still being done and truth be told, I am still learning. I did, however, pick up great pieces of advice for how you can go from feeling worthless, imprisoned, and isolated, to finding joy, love, and acceptance. All I ever wanted was to be accepted and love growing up like any other child. This was not my experience and perhaps it was not yours either.

Maybe your childhood is littered with rejection, isolation, judgment, hatred, and self loathing. I didn't like myself because I was not what everyone else expected me to be. You wouldn't think the way you were born, how you adapted to life naturally would cause so much of a fuss for others; I learned that it can. Being on the receiving end of this harsh judgment can create some behavioral patterns that need to be tweaked if you want to be free to love and be loved.

      I want to help you know that you deserve the love you crave. You deserve to have someone love you for who you are, with flaws and all. No one is perfect and the perfection that you feel compelled to deliver to be loved, I want to show you is unjustified. You were not born to be perfect, you are imperfectly perfect to live out your purpose. You can choose to work out your purpose smarter and not harder by allowing me to give you shortcuts to the road of increased self worth.

Introduction

Have you ever wondered why you behave the way you do and respond in the manner you do? Have you noticed a recurring pattern in your choices? Do you wonder why you attract the same type of friends or partners? They may have different names, but the characters, behavior, and outcomes remain the same. That was me until I started a journey of self-discovery.

The journey began when my therapist asked me if I had suffered abuse as a child, and I said "no." You see, I did not have the full context of what child abuse was. I had assumed child abuse was starving, hitting, or severaly beating a child and of which none had happened to me. I had my definition, and what I had endured as a child simply did not fit that framework. Emotional, verbal, and mental abuse never occurred to me as a form of abuse. Have you ever suffered in silence and didn't know what you survived until you were on the other side?

Born left-handed in a part of the world where it is deemed taboo, I faced numerous challenges. Child emotional maltreatment was not recognized, and I was left with no protection from the discrimination I encountered simply for being different. It is ironic that in a world filled with billions of people we can even imagine there is a so-called normal when each of us are uniquely and wonderfully made.

In the society I grew up in, extending my left hand in greeting or offering assistance was considered disrespectful, unclean, and extremely offensive. Despite my left hand being my dominant hand, using it carried such a negative connotation. Can you imagine the feeling of thinking you are wrong, vile, and rejected because of something you could not help? People didn't offer to help me, but instead separated and isolated themselves from me. This separation made me feel terrible about the girl and woman I would someday grow up to become.

I could not even catch a break outside my home and school. My left-handedness seemed to displease everyone I interacted with even strangers. Grocery attendants would not give me back my change if I accidentally extended my left hand to receive it. Whenever I sat to eat with my peers, they would chastise me vehemently for dipping my left hand into the shared bowl of food. They would give me ultimatums to either use my right hand or leave!

I felt so ashamed and I learned techniques to cope with my problem, which honestly should not have been an issue at all. I said no one tried to help me, but more accurately I should say they attempted to assist me in "correcting" my left-handedness–except my father. I will further explain his role later in the book. I was repeatedly reminded, often through being slapped and at times spanked, to use my right hand when performing tasks, like offering water to visiting family members. Again, spankings were normal where I am from so child abuse would mean near death experiences often.

You may ask, did your teachers try to help you sort out your feelings or a guidance counselor? Even my teachers did not excuse me and would harshly punish me if they caught me writing with my left hand. They demanded that I use my right hand and their constant admonitions were to "Use your right hand, child!" In addition to my left-handed troubles, I also suffered from nocturnal enuresis. I was a bedwetter, the only one among my siblings. Left-handed and a bed wetter; it could not be worse. My life was hell. I felt as though I was cursed and an outcast in my own family. I felt different, unloved, unaccepted, isolated, and unworthy.

As a vulnerable child, my already low self-esteem suffered a critical blow inflicted by a caregiver (who happened to be a close family member.) This individual constantly told me I was ugly and the least attractive among my siblings. Unfortunately, I internalized her hurtful words and allowed them to shape my thoughts about me. These experiences formed my mindset early in life, reinforcing my belief that I was unlovable, unacceptable, unworthy, and undeserving of anything nice or of value. I carried this survival blueprint into my adult life, and it played a critical role in my relationship choices.

Through my experiences, I now understand that individuals who have faced neglect, abuse, loss, or have felt imperfect, undesirable, unlovable, or different, often struggle to accept and welcome love into their lives. As children, our biological makeup and brains attempt to process negative experiences by creating harmful coping mechanisms. These negative mechanisms become deeply ingrained in our survival blueprints. Certain situations, such as a disagreement with a partner, a rejection for a job, or harsh comments can trigger those deep set emotions later in life. As these emotions evolve, they can result in a cascade of negativity including shame, loneliness, feelings of inadequacy, rejection, abandonment, mistrust, and more.

Childhood experiences play a critical role in shaping who we are as adults. Traumatic events in childhood can leave lasting impacts on our emotional and psychological well-being that can manifest in our relationships and life choices. In this book, I explore how childhood traumas can influence adult relationships, from romantic partnerships to friendships and family connections. I also dig into how childhood traumas can shape our choices in life, including career paths, hobbies, and even our worldview. Through personal stories and experiences, scientific research, and expert insights, I endeavor to shed light on the often-unseen impact of childhood traumas on our adult lives.

I invite you to join me on an exploratory journey. Together, we can delve into how past experiences influence our present behaviors and attitudes in romantic relationships. Understanding this truth can be a powerful tool for personal growth and self-awareness. By exploring our attachment patterns and behaviors, we can gain insight into why we struggle in certain areas of our relationships and learn how to create healthier, more fulfilling relationships in the future.

Chapter 1
The Burden of Being Different: Searching for Validation

No one really understands what it means to be different like those of us who have been black sheeps of the family. When I relocated to America my culture wasn't different from yours. Raised with a British influence I know all too well what it means to be the black sheep of the family. A more coined term in the US, is being treated like a red-headed stepchild. That wasn't a saying I knew, but I quickly learned that I identified with the concept. Just as much as I identify with the slang of being treated like a read-headed stepchild and the coined term middle-child syndrome.

For those of us who have been left out of conversations, ignored when we showed our face, or people turned away our helping hand, we know what it feels like to be rejected. The pain and the shame can be unbearable at times. So much so, many of us create systems for dealing and avoiding such sorrow. I realized, I chased after validation, because I was living with the burden of being different.

I felt like a social outcast because I was different and did not meet the standards for what my culture deemed normal. I was born left-handed in a right-hand society. The very simple notion of me living seemed to bother people that were dear to me.

It hurt my heart for years to think about my childhood and how I grew up. I didn't want to believe it mattered as much as it did. It pained me to start this journey of self discovery because it meant I had to relive some of my most traumatic experiences. I can imagine you may feel like I did. In that you know there is a problem in you being a black sheep. You have an idea for how it negatively impacted your decisions and the thoughts you have about yourself. The next question you likely have is, what can I do about it?

Discussing adverse childhood experiences can be challenging and unsettling. I know talking about it is probably the last thing you want to do. It could feel like navigating through a pitch-dark room, searching for something hidden. But I assure you this process is necessary and you will thank me, same as I thanked another.

Acknowledging and shedding light on these experiences may be very difficult for most of us, however, the process is crucial to healing. I am no expert, but I am a coach on how to show people how to do what I have done to get victory over my childhood trauma and I want to share these tips with you. By gaining a deeper understanding of how childhood trauma can present itself, we can begin to address the root causes and work toward healing and recovery.

It is important to recognize that the effects of childhood trauma can vary widely and may manifest in different ways. For me, validation became everything to me. I constantly looked for other people to tell me I was good enough although I had already given myself the answer. My answer was always, "No, you are not good enough, deserving, beautiful, or accepted."

Have you told yourself similar things? Outloud, in your mind, within your thoughts? Working with my clients, I realized some people may struggle with anxiety or depression. Clinical depression is a real thing and a necessary issue to take a look at. Although medication may be needed to cope, don't rely solely on medicine to do the work you will have to do personally to aid the process. I have been to therapy and I knew the true work began when I started to implement what I was hearing and learning.

I got to a point where I really did need someone to walk with me in this dark room as I searched through my things. The truth is, I was afraid to find myself, and I treated myself how others had, I distanced myself and tried to move on without her.

Some of you may develop self-destructive behaviors such as substance abuse or an eating disorder. It is not uncommon for individuals who have experienced trauma in childhood to have difficulty forming healthy relationships or trusting others especially as adults. To be honest, I had issues selecting healthy relationships for myself before starting this journey. The best relationships I have now, are the ones I trusted God to pick for me. I love all of my children and genuine friends who stuck with me as I learned and accepted me.

In all these cases, even ones I haven't mentioned, we all may struggle with shame, guilt, and low self-worth. . It takes courage and vulnerability to confront the pain of our past. As we confront our past, we learn that we can start processing our emotions and rebuilding our sense of self. By shining a light on our experiences, we are no longer in the dark, and we can find what was hidden easily because we can identify patterns and triggers that may be impacting our current behaviors and work towards developing healthy coping mechanisms.

It takes courage and vulnerability to confront the pain of our past. In doing so, however, we can start processing our emotions and rebuilding our sense of self.

I have learnt that childhood trauma comes in many different shapes and sizes. For some, it might feel like they were not wanted or loved. It could involve extreme violence, abuse, or neglect. Also not uncommon are individuals who have been made to feel less than because they were excluded or told they were inadequate. Strangers are not often the culprits for these traumatic experiences, parents with unresolved emotional wounds are very guilty of spreading their trauma with their children.

No matter what form trauma takes, it always leaves a mark. You and I, victims, develop coping mechanisms to deal with our negative experiences, and its effects on our mental and emotional health can lead to a wide range of symptoms. I've learned and accepted, every child is born unique, with the traits and characteristics that make them who they are. As one of over 130 million newborns welcomed the year of my birth, it was fascinating that I came into the world with my unique makeup.

Yet, growing up left-handed was a source of constant frustration and shame for me. I was made to feel like an outcast and an aberration that needed to be "fixed." It was as if I had committed a grave mistake by not conforming to the norm of being right-handed. Before I realized I was a giant, one born with purpose, big dreams, hopes, and aspirations, I believed I was a mistake.

My family and caregivers were quick to admonish me whenever I used my left hand to do anything. Even simple tasks like eating or writing were met with disapproval and scolding. I was told that using my left hand was wrong and that I needed to use my right hand instead. I was left feeling confused and ashamed, wondering why my left-handedness was something to be frowned upon. I did not understand why I deserved the treatment I received. All I knew was that I was different and different was not a good thing.

To avoid the disapproval and scolding that came with using my left hand, I did my best to conform to the expectations of those around me. I tried to use my right hand for everything, even though it felt awkward and uncomfortable. I consistently experienced a sense of displacement and the feeling that I did not belong. The fear of making mistakes and being judged for them kept me in a constant state of anxiety, which hindered my ability to cultivate a sense of self-confidence.

Despite my best efforts to conform, I could not shake the feeling that something was inherently wrong with me. I spent a lot of energy trying to change myself to please others and fit in with the crowd. At an early age, I learned to please people and sought validation from others. I longed for acceptance and to be loved for who I was, but the constant admonishment for being left-handed made me feel broken and unworthy. It was not until much later in life that I realized how damaging this behavior was and how it had robbed me of my individuality and self esteem.

As I transitioned from that little innocent girl to womanhood, a deep, unhealthy need for validation took hold of me. I no longer had a standard for what I deserved. The result was a long-complicated pattern of toxic romantic choices, self-sabotage, and unhappiness. Are you searching for validation in all the wrong places like me? Did you marry the wrong person, you feel? Are you pursuing someone now that you know you shouldn't but can't help yourself?

You are not attracted to the bad things because you are crazy, stupid, or dumb. You are leaning on your coping mechanisms that are ingrained in you as a child and you are fighting those ideas as you read this book and look at your life choices. Don't get discouraged because you see a fault in your stars, allow the desire to improve your life, push you to keep reading.

The painful experiences I lived through taught me how to adapt and survive in a world that often values conformity over individuality. You are very normal, because it is sad to say, but trauma and pain are normal facets of life. However, you should not maintain coping mechanisms when you have the chance to heal and be restored. When you break a limb, you get a cast, after the cast comes off, you expect to be healed and go back to full use of your limb. How often do we get hurt and live our lifetime in a cast, or worse in a sling when we should have gotten a cast, all to live a limited life because of our experiences and pain.

Looking back, I now understand that the negative attitudes towards left-handedness were passed down from generation to generation without much thought or understanding. My parents did their best to raise a child that society would accept. Despite the best intentions, they inadvertently made me feel broken and unworthy.

Throughout my journey of self-discovery, I have come to realize that my experiences are not uncommon. Many individuals have gone through similar situations growing up, resulting in feelings of inadequacy and a belief that their lives hold no value. These individuals often struggle with various challenges, such as codependency and a lack of self worth. Feeling unworthy can lead to mental health symptoms such as anxiety, depression, addiction, trauma, impostor syndrome, and relationship issues.

What I want to show you that I learned, acknowledging and embracing our uniqueness, we can learn to love and accept ourselves for who we truly are. This self-acceptance can be a powerful tool in overcoming our challenges and achieving personal growth. By recognizing that our experiences and perspectives are valuable, we can build a sense of self-worth that can positively impact all aspects of our lives.

What I want you to see, is that thing about you that others wanted you to change to fit the norm, may be something that makes you unique. I am not debating right or wrong, but me being left handed was not a sin but a uniqueness God gave me. I want you to take a moment and think about something that makes you unique. This can be something others told you was not valuable, necessary, or was a character flaw.

I want you to picture it, see it in your mind's eye, and know it makes you unique. There is no such thing as perfect. We are all wonderfully made and need different things as we were born for different reasons. Don't put so much pressure on yourself to be someone else, you can only be you and don't be ashamed of that.

In my experience, as I began to explore and accept myself, I discovered that being left-handed was simply a part of who I was. It was a unique and valuable aspect of my identity that set me apart from others in a positive way. I realized there was no reason to be ashamed or to hide this aspect of myself from the world.

I have since learned to embrace my individuality and to celebrate the things that make me unique. Each of us has a set of characteristics and experiences that contribute to who we are. It is only by accepting and celebrating these differences that we can truly live fulfilling and authentic lives.

I am grateful for the experience, as it has taught me the importance of self-acceptance and the dangers of trying to change oneself to please others. In the past, I hid my identity, feelings, expectations, and desires to conform to society's or a partner's expectations. In doing so, I had denied an essential part of myself. I had sacrificed my own needs and desires to fit in with the expectations of others. In the end, I only succeeded in making myself miserable.

Reflecting on my past struggles with self-acceptance and embracing my unique characteristics, I have come to a place of gratitude for the experience. I have learned that the road to self-acceptance can be difficult, but the rewards are immeasurable. Instead of feeling ashamed or inadequate because of my left-handedness, I celebrate it as a fundamental part of my identity.

> I had sacrificed my own needs and desires to fit in with the expectations of others. In the end, I only succeeded in making myself miserable.

I believe everyone should embrace their individuality, regardless of what form it may take. Our differences are what make us unique and special, and we should celebrate them rather than try to conform to societal norms. I hope that my experience can serve as inspiration for you to embrace your individuality and know that you are not alone in this journey. I am here to help coach you through it!

Remember, healing from childhood trauma is a journey that cannot be rushed or completed overnight. By taking the first step of acknowledging and exploring our past experiences, we can break free from the cycle of trauma and begin to build a brighter future for ourselves and the diverse world we can help to create. If you allow me to help you do the work, we can create a diverse world of accepting people, moving with the same passion, to cultivate healthy relationships with others for a more fulfilling life

Think Points:
1. Do you feel growing up you were affirmed and supported by your parents and family?
2. In your current relationship, do you feel you are jumping through hoops to show your affection? Is that same energy reciprocal?
3. Do you see a pattern, that you are wanting to please people even if that means hurting yourself?
4. Are you comfortable saying "no"?

Changes can take place slowly or swiftly. Be open to allow your choices to take their natural pace. Sometimes the best thing you can do is give yourself time. I want you to take the time you need but think about the sacrifices you are making or have made.

Exercise: Now I want you to do a simple exercise. I want you to write down your answer to this question: What changes do you want to make moving forward?

_____

_____

_____

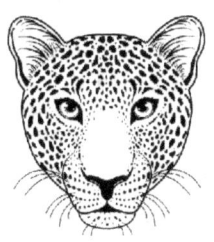

Chapter 2
How Childhood Experiences Manifest In Adult Relationships

I want you to be honest, "Are you a toxic relationship magnet?" Have you set out to build relationships, romantic or friendships and found you attract similar people over and over again? They have a different face, personality, but they soon become someone you want to get away from. You think, "What is wrong with these people and how do they keep finding me?" At least I used to, but I did see eventually there was a common denominator, me.

I had to do some soul searching to find the answers to my questions. Our childhood experiences play a significant role in our adult lives, including our choices of romantic partners or even friends. What happens to us in childhood shapes our beliefs, values, and behaviors, which then influence how we approach relationships. For instance, if we experience neglect or abandonment as children, we may struggle with trust issues and find it hard to form healthy attachments with others. Similarly, if we witness unhealthy dynamics between our parents or caregivers, we may unknowingly repeat those patterns in our relationships.

Recognizing what role our childhood experiences play in our adult lives is key to understanding ourselves and making conscious choices about the types of relationships we want to cultivate. Negative experiences often leave deep emotional wounds that may persist into adulthood. The impact of such adversity can manifest in various ways, such as our capacity for self love, trust, and intimacy. Because my childhood was marked by emotional turmoil and instability, I struggled with trust issues. My past influenced my choices when it came to romantic partners and friends. I found myself gravitating toward people who were emotionally unavailable or who ended up hurting me. It was not until I started working through my past trauma that I was able to break free from these patterns and start forming healthier relationships.

My past influenced my choices when it came to romantic partners and friends. I found myself gravitating toward people who were emotionally unavailable or who ended up

hurting me.

Are you currently going against the grain of your own happiness? Do you make decisions that are counterproductive to what you want to have, be, or become? I used to be just like you and I believed I deserved it. I didn't blame others, even when it was their fault, I was used to being the problem. I believed all problems started with me and even worse, I felt a need to solve them.

Are you taking on other people's problems? Are you burning your candle at both ends and know sooner or later, you are going to be melted laying on a table because there is nothing left! I want to stop you from doing what I did, but also encourage you if your road is similar.

During one of my therapy sessions, my therapist asked me a challenging question that left a lasting impression on me. She asked, "Would you recognize love if you met it on the streets?" At first, I was taken aback by her question. I asked myself two internal questions that I am glad I didn't voice, *What did she mean? Was she insinuating that I was incapable of embracing love?* Before I could shift gears from being slightly offended to getting mad, she elaborated. I began to understand what she meant. Her question was not to offend me but to bring attention to a potential obstacle in my path toward emotional well-being.

Have you ever blown up on the wrong person because they asked a question that honestly you should have asked yourself? Do you have an accountability partner, coach, or therapist, you can be real with? I realized I was fake for so long I didn't recognize it anymore and the main person that was missing out was me. I thought by hiding I was escaping only to find I was dragging my baggage with me.

My therapist explained that the pain and brokenness I experienced during childhood had impacted my ability to recognize true love. It was a stab in the heart to realize the relationships and the emotions I had were not organic love. In fact, I didn't know what love really was in the scope of romantic relationships. I managed to pick great friends, and have wonderful relationships with my children, but I did have to face my fallacy of love when it came to my romantic life.

Every runaway bride soon has to stop running and give an account on her decision to leave the altar. No matter the reason, you will have to at minimum answer yourself if no one else. I had to face Kemi in the mirror, and reason with her because she was the one I owed an answer. Kemi, do you know what love is? Then, can I give something I don't have for myself to someone else?

We are able to fake an array of things, but love

is something you cannot fake once you know what it is. It is not a word, an emotion, or a fabrication, it is a moving and living, powerful force that will make you long-suffering. Give your time, attention, patience, and care. You will have a tender heart towards the person because we cannot love things. Things are not made with the capability of sharing love only receiving worship, attention, and likes. True love is given and received by parties.

I remember the feeling I had as I sat on the couch. It was as if a veil had been cast over my eyes, preventing me from seeing and experiencing love in its purest form. Without addressing these underlying issues, I would continue to make poor relationship choices and remain trapped in a cycle of chaos and temporary happiness.

The messages I received about myself growing up convinced me that I was not as good as other people and was inferior to others.

This realization was difficult to accept, but also a turning point in my healing journey. Through therapy, I learned to identify and address the wounds from my past, allowing myself to approach relationships with a renewed sense of clarity and understanding. While the healing process can be challenging, it is also empowering to know that we have the ability to heal and grow, no matter how deep our wounds may be.

As I mentioned earlier, my struggles began long before I started dating. The messages I received about myself growing up convinced me that I was not as good as other people and was inferior to others. It ingrained in me that my value depended on being just like, or even better than, everyone else.

Unfortunately, I did not realize until later that a genuine connection with someone requires mutual acceptance and appreciation of each other, flaws and all. By the time I started pursuing romantic relationships, I had already developed this misguided idea that my left-handedness and appearance made me imperfect, unlovable. I felt like something was wrong with me and that my partner held the key to my emotional well-being.

To put it simply, I gave my partners the power to control my life like a TV remote. Whatever they felt was best, I believed was best. I sought to please him even if I was displeased. I let them switch me on and off and even change my channels. There were dreams I had, that I put on hold because I didn't see how they fit into the script my partner wrote. As a result, my relationships were a wild roller coaster of emotions with me being dragged in every which way.

I had emotional whiplash and my body, heart,

and mind responded to the pain. I became hyper alert and tried to remain 5 steps ahead of everyone else. My sense of overachievement was not born out of a desire to be great, but to avoid being punished. Due to my emotional instability, I struggled with bedwetting for a long time when I was younger.

I lived in constant fear of making mistakes and being punished. Being prone to anxiety and having a strong desire to please others, I became a perfectionist in everything I did. While my classmates put in minimal effort, I went above and beyond to ensure that nothing would give anyone a reason to punish me.

As I grew older, these tendencies persisted and manifested in other ways. Despite appearing confident on the outside, I had very low self-esteem and constantly sought validation from others. I would go to great lengths to outdo my peers and earn their approval–even if it meant compromising my standards or accepting mistreatment from others.

In the romance arena, I consistently found myself attracting partners who mirrored the negative beliefs I had about myself. I was not aware at the time, but I sought out individuals who treated me poorly and made me feel unworthy as I believed it was all I deserved. I tended to choose partners who were emotionally unavailable or talked down to me using mean statements.

The sad part was I expected and accepted them calling me (insert names) and I gave them permission. Are you giving people permission to abuse you? To call you terrible names and reassure an old belief that needs to be removed from your mind and heart? If you were like me, you are trying to please others hoping to win their love and approval. When things went wrong, I blamed myself and made excuses for their bad behavior.

Are you covering up the terrible actions others are doing and allowing old patterns to be further ingrained into your psyche? I want to encourage you like I too needed encouragement while struggling to break free from relationships like these. Due to my low self-esteem, I was willing to accept anything from my partners, even if it was disrespectful or insufficient, as long as it meant they would love me in return. I had no standards for choosing romantic partners. I overlooked significant flaws in them as long as they claimed to love me. I saw myself as undeserving of love and affection, and this lack of self-worth manifested in my relationships.

Looking back, I realize that my childhood experiences taught me that love was a transactional exchange. I believed that I had to earn love by constantly pleasing others and that if I failed, I would be punished or rejected. This mindset was toxic and led to a lot of disappointment and heartache. The belief system carried over into my adult life. It took me a long time to learn that true love and self-worth come from within, not through external validation.

It was when I began to address these underlying beliefs and patterns in therapy I was able to make positive changes in my life. I learned to establish healthy boundaries, prioritize self-worth, respect, and pursue relationships built on mutual love rather than ones driven by fear or obligation.

Through this process, I also learned that the love and acceptance I had sought from others could only come from within. I started to practice self-compassion and self-care. Gradually, I began to build a stronger sense of self-worth. It is vital to understand that childhood experiences significantly impact our personalities and attitudes toward various aspects of life, including how we approach romantic relationships and friendships.

Something I noticed, we tend to attract individuals who mirror our inner selves. How we grew up is a vital factor in shaping our choices in partners and how we interact in relationships. These early experiences shape our beliefs, values, and behaviors, which can affect our ability to form healthy and fulfilling relationships in the future. Understanding how childhood trauma shapes our attitudes and behaviors can help us identify and address any negative patterns hindering our personal growth and well-being.

Through this process, I also learned that the love and acceptance I had sought from others could only come from within. I started to practice self-compassion and self-care. Gradually, I began to build a stronger sense of self-worth.

Let me provide an anecdote to illustrate this phenomenon. A close acquaintance and (frequent visitor in my coaching circle) recipient of my coaching grew up in a household where her father, a Nigerian military officer, would bring his girlfriends home. Her mother would dutifully cook for them both and not appear to be bothered. Growing up in this environment, my friend accepted this conduct as normal behavior.

Clearly, this upbringing would reasonably have a lasting impact on her attitudes toward relationships in her adult life. She was open to being involved with someone already in a committed relationship including marriage. She saw nothing wrong in being the "other woman." This example highlights how childhood experiences can impact our attitudes and behaviors in adulthood.

Allow me to share another example. A close family member repeatedly told me I was the ugliest of all my siblings. She would constantly say this to me, even when reprimanding me for something I did wrong. No matter the problem, being ugly was the angle she started and ended with. Fast forward to when I was attending university in Nigeria.

I had a good friend who was on the organizing committee for the university's pageant. She approached me a few times and said she needed to talk to me. We finally got a chance to speak, and she said they had four candidates, and she wanted me to be the fifth. I was taken aback and told her I needed to think about it. She urged me to let her know as soon as possible, so she could tell the organizers.

When I returned to my room, I was upset and told my roommate what had happened. She did not understand why I was so upset and asked me to explain. I explained that I did not want to be in a beauty pageant because I knew I was not beautiful. I certainly did not appreciate being mocked by my acquaintance inviting me to join something I thought I did not qualify for.

My roommate was puzzled and did not understand why I felt disqualified. She told me that I was beautiful. That was a new concept! I did not see myself the way she saw me. How could I? I had been ingrained with the belief that I was ugly from a young age. Hearing my roommate's words gave me a glimmer of hope. Maybe they were right. Perhaps I was not as ugly as I thought. From that day on, I felt different and I no longer saw myself as an ugly duckling.

Another example is a friend whose parents had only one bank account for the entire family. This example from her parents molded her financial perspective. It resulted in her resisting the suggestion of creating individual accounts when her spouse proposed it. She saw the division as a separation and a break in their bond, while he didn't see it that way at all. Some of the simplest things to some can be a landmine for others when crossed.

These examples illustrate how childhood experiences influence our romantic relationships, friendships, and other relationships. It is crucial to reflect on our past and how it may impact our current behavior and decision-making. By acknowledging our beliefs and attitudes by making conscious choices, we can break free from patterns that no longer serve us and foster healthier relationships.

While the effects of my childhood experiences still impact me to this day, I am proud of the progress I have made and the person I have become. I also know that I am not defined by my past. With time and effort, I continue to grow and evolve and I am determined to help others do the same. Coaching, speaking, and mentoring is not about having people look at me because I have all the answers, but because I have taken the journey and I know what I need to change and sustain my life. I decided to become what I wanted for others and advocate.

I deserve to be treated with care, respect, and dignity. I do not have to settle for less than that in a partner.

Now I am able to approach relationships and life more positively and healthily. I am grateful for the lessons I have learned along the way to better my relationships. I have learned that love is not transactional but a mutual exchange of care and support. I deserve to be treated with care, respect, and dignity. I do not have to settle for less than that in a partner.

I have learned to set boundaries that I encourage you to take a moment to envision. I want you to consider the people, thoughts, or ideas that are a threat to you having healthy boundaries. Loving people should not mean you have no standards. Helping people can coexist with self-care and self-love. It is okay to prioritize your wants, desires in a partner and you don't have to say, yes because they did..

You are important and you don't have to beg to be accepted, loved, or appreciated. The right person for you will wilfully give you love, attention, and care. Just be sure you give love back to the people who deserve it also. I had to learn to love the people that loved me and not just the ones I wanted to love me.

I know this is not an easy process, it took time and effort to change my old patterns of behavior. But gradually, I began to see positive changes in my relationships. I learned to say, "No!" when something did not feel right. I started to attract people who were kind and respectful. I no longer felt the need to please others at the expense of my own well-being.

Today, I am in a loving and healthy relationship and I know I deserve nothing less.

Think Point:
1. How are you feeling after reading this chapter?
2. Do you feel like counseling may be something you can benefit from? Or, have you been to counseling already?
3. During the process, or after attending, do you feel like there is still room for you to grow?
4. Are there patterns you would like to change and if so which ones? Now, do you have a

plan for change?

Exercise: I want you to do a Life Check-In and ask yourself 3 simple questions.
- How do I feel right now?
- What has happened that made me feel this way?
- Why am I responding like I am?

_____
_____
_____
_____
_____
_____
_____
_____
_____
_____
_____
_____
_____
_____

_____

_____

_____

_____

    If you realize the source of the issue that is a great sign. If you do not know the source of your pain, then we should connect to determine what it is exactly. Not knowing how you feel or why you are feeling a certain way, can make you uncomfortable. I want you to know this is normal, and a breakthrough call is what you need.

Visit KemiSpeaks.com to schedule or Scan the QR code for additional contact details

Kemi Speaks

Chapter 3
Befriending Fear

Fear or flight is a concept we have all studied in psych courses. We know the concept but we don't always see how the implication impacts our real life. It makes sense that when we are afraid our brain tells us to fight and protect ourselves or run when facing a bear, spiders, or trauma. Yet when we are faced with fear many of us have taken refuge in fear.

How so? When we are faced with our deepest fears, thoughts, imaginations we don't run from the thoughts. When we think we are ugly and hear someone call us that, we don't fight the person, nor run away from them, but we befriend, love, and even marry them! Do you think it odd you pick people that do not care for you, show you love or respect, but you pursue the relationship?

This person can ignore you for days on end

and instead of you celebrating their absence, you wonder, what did I do wrong for them to avoid me. If they call you names, instead of getting away from them quick, fast and in a hurry, you think, they must be having a bad day or you feel they are telling the truth.

You don't fight, but fear has disarmed you, and worse still became your friend. In this chapter, I want us to explore the concept of befriending fear and overcoming the lingering effects of childhood fears. Like with anything, something that took you years to learn, can take time to see. I want you to be patient with me in this chapter because you can pivot your life if you continue to read with an open mind.

So far, I have only talked about relationships you choose but what about the ones you are born into? What about the family members you have that you cannot get away from or toss out of your life because they are rude, mean, and cruel? Many of us know that one cousin, uncle, sibling, or parent that is just mean.

We may speculate why they treat us like they do, but the truth, does the reason ever justify the cruel treatment of someone else? I would argue it does not. My father was the only person growing up that could understand me. He was also a lefty like me.

Growing up I remember him saying, "Just let her be!" He always tried to defend me and shield me from the disapproving looks and comments that were watered down for me than what he experienced. I cannot fathom what he went through when times were even more cruel toward left handed people.

I could only imagine his pain, and that of those you love too, who want to save you but cannot. They want to shelter you from all harm and danger, only their arms don't stretch wide enough and their voice t does not drown out the world. My father, I know, felt helpless to change the country and culture in which we were born and raised.

He and my mother did not stay together until death did them part, but a part of me died when he left. I felt abandoned, isolated, and without a person that could really be in my corner. It seemed like everyone picked a side and the side was not mine. I was a child, alone, fighting for my right to be me, like my father. He was my only sense of normal and he was gone.

I was heartbroken when he left for more than one reason. Perhaps, my reason was selfish at the core, but well intended. No one wants to be alone in the world. We were all made to live in community with each other. It is a dark place to be alone and fear can easily become your friend when you have no refuge from it.

I lived in constant fear of disappointing people I loved. I believed they loved me, but it was very hard to tell. I felt judged and misunderstood more than love. Out of fear I ran to over deliver in every way possible. Fear became my motivator and turned me into an overachiever. I became my best and worst enemy.

From a tender age we are conditioned to perceive fear as an undesirable, icky, and uncomfortable emotion. We are taught to evade it, overcome it, or even disregard it entirely. But what if I told you that fear can be repurposed to be your friend, a helpful ally? What if befriending fear could serve as the solution to unlocking your maximum potential?

For most of us, fear and anxiety were constant companions in our childhood homes, and these emotions followed us into adulthood. The worries of parents or caretakers about various matters, such as finances or safety, left a lasting impression on us. We learned to be fearful from an early age. Caution and avoidance of potential dangers were instilled in us early in life. Our concerned and caring caregivers often told us to be careful, to watch out, and to avoid danger. The result was that we adopted fear traits.

A case in point is my use of the left hand

instead of the right. It may seem insignificant, but it can reveal a lot about our subconscious fears and beliefs. Growing up, I was afraid of making mistakes, presenting my dominant left hand instead of my right hand. I felt I was doing things the wrong way and taking unnecessary risks when being different. This fear became a stumbling block just as much as it was a motivator. Even though I achieved a certain level of success, it kept me from reaching my full potential of living the life I truly wanted.

> For most of us, fear and anxiety were constant companions in our childhood homes, and these emotions followed us into adulthood.

As adults, the DNA of fear imprinted on us through childhood experiences manifests as anxiety and hypervigilance. We are often on the lookout for potential threats or situations that could lead to negative consequences. We are constantly having these inner talks that are fear driven.

"What if I wear this dress and I am overdressed? Won't my friends think I am trying to upstage them?"

"I think I have a solution, but what happens if I speak up and it is a dumb idea? Let me be safe and keep quiet."

If you don't believe it yet, you will see how

much fear can be a powerful motivator in your life. By fear, people who love us say, "You need to get married, you're not getting any younger." Or, "I worry about you being alone, don't you think it is time to get back in the saddle and date again?"

Fear can make you agree with others as you make decisions about relationships and marriage. Making life altering choices in this state of mind can lead us to make choices that are not in our best interests. For instance, as a woman, the fear of our biological clock ticking may pressure us to settle for a partner who may not be the best match for us. Similarly, the fear of ending up alone or not being able to find someone else can cause us to say yes to situations or people that we know deep down are wrong for us.

Fear can bully us to say yes when we should say no. It can make us say yes to proposals that we know are unsuitable because we fear missing out on a chance for companionship. This terrible foe often in our lives seems to shine a laser light to our deepest insecurities. How quickly fear can switch sides and go from good to bad help is astonishing.

Some people have adopted the philosophy, 'I would rather be with him/her than be alone.' This fear of loneliness can cause people to overlook important aspects of relationships like compatibility and mutual respect. They may feel like a safe or easy choice, but in the long run, they can limit our potential and prevent us from living the life we truly want and deserve. It can also lead to feelings of regret, resentment, or dissatisfaction. Do not settle for less than what you deserve.

> You see, fear can be a powerful motivator in our lives. It even shows up in our decisions about relationships and marriage leading us to make choices that are not in our best interests.

What is essential is taking the time to find someone who is truly compatible and who shares similar values and goals. It is fear that makes us people pleasers. We fear rejection or being ostracized if we do not go with the crowd. As a result, we hide how we really feel or put up with mistreatment or bad behavior from others. Fear can also manifest itself in romantic relationships. The following are some ways in which it negatively affects romantic relationships:

Insecurity: Fear can manifest as insecurity in a relationship. An individual may fear that their partner will leave, cheat on them, or find someone better. This insecurity can cause them to act possessive, jealous, and controlling. This behavior can erode trust and ultimately push their partner away.

Fear of commitment: Fear of commitment can prevent people from fully investing in their relationships. This fear may stem from past experiences of being hurt or betrayed, and it can cause people to avoid long-term relationships. For example, someone afraid of commitment may avoid making plans with their partner or shy away from discussing their long-term goals.

Fear of abandonment: This can lead to clingy or needy behavior in relationships. This fear may stem from past experiences of being abandoned or neglected, and it can cause people to fear being left alone. For example, someone afraid of abandonment may constantly seek reassurance from their partner or become upset when their partner spends time with others.

Lack of vulnerability: Fear can cause individuals to avoid being vulnerable in their relationships. They may be hesitant to share their deepest feelings and thoughts with their partner out of fear of being judged or rejected. This lack of vulnerability can lead to a lack of emotional intimacy, which can ultimately damage the relationship and even end it prematurely.

Sabotaging behavior: Fear can also lead to self-sabotaging behavior in a relationship. An individual may fear being hurt or rejected and, as a result, push their partner away or create problems in the relationship. This behavior can damage the relationship and make it difficult for both partners to feel secure and happy.

Fear of intimacy: Fear of intimacy can prevent people from fully connecting with their partners. This fear may stem from past traumas or negative experiences. Someone afraid of intimacy may avoid physical touch or emotional vulnerability with their partner.

The good news is that we can work through our fears and learn to make choices that are truly aligned with our values and desires. We should not allow fear to control our choices. When we befriend fear by facing it head-on and understanding where it can motivate us, we level up. In doing so, we gain a sense of control over our lives and make choices that lead to greater happiness and fulfillment.

If we navigate through our fear and develop a stronger sense of self-worth, we will find that we can make decisions that align better with our true desires and values. We can start to see fear for what it is, a transient emotion, and begin to move beyond it. Fear can be a powerful force in our lives, but it does not have to be the only factor influencing our choices.

The key message here is that we must acknowledge fear without allowing it to control our decision-making. Fear is a temporary emotion that should not hold us back from taking necessary risks or making informed choices. Although it may have been deeply implanted in us since childhood, we should take the time to unpack it by asking ourselves the right questions. Why am I afraid? What is it about this situation that makes me feel unsettled? Why does this behavior or words trigger this emotion in me?

I know that working through our fears is not always easy or comfortable. It may require us to confront difficult emotions, question long-held beliefs, or step outside our comfort zones, but the rewards are worth it. By facing our fears and doing the necessary self-work, we can become more resilient and confident and attract healthy relationships.

Think Points
1. When you think of fear, do you see it as mostly a negative term?
2. Do you feel that fear has motivated you to make life changes and if so, what choices?
3. Is fear motivating you toward healthy lifestyle decisions or crippling your journey?
4. In what ways do you feel a renewed relationship with fear, even if that means removing

fear, can help you make better choices?

We can have a renewed relationship with fear that benefits us. I had to implement techniques that opened my mind and removed limiting ideas and behaviors. I want to encourage you now to try something. I want you to pretend there are no limits and anything you can write, envision, and speak, you can have!

Exercise: As you think about these questions, I want you to write about the life you want. I want you to write out what your family looks like. How often you see them. Where you live and how you live. Now, I want you to look at the fear you may have that says, "You can't do that." Encourage yourself and say, "Yes, I can." Write your vision and end it with, "Yes, I can get this!"

_____

_____

_____

_____

_____

_____

_____

_____

_____

_____

_____

Chapter 4
Know Yourself

Can you relate to the reports that 45% of women will not get married or ever have children by the year 2050? I am not sure how true this is and what the stats demonstrate. Do they demonstrate women are growing increasingly less interested in romantic affairs?

Does it point to the truth that many women would rather build their careers and accomplish success over having a family? Or could it point to a more sinister reality, many of us are struggling with selecting, keeping, or staying in healthy relationships?

Do you live with the statistical proof that divorce accounts for the life cycle for about 51% of marriages. In America, and really all around the world, the stigma of divorce is shifting as this old taboo becomes less important. It hasn't lost all its power because many of us get married and keep on getting married even when we are not ready to avoid the judgment.

The women that have it the worst are those who have lived through toxic relationships or who have poorly defined relationships to love. For the many of us trying to pull together a marriage or dating experience from tainted love, we struggle more than any other group. It is no wonder why some of us give up on finding the ideal man we dream of.

It should not be shocking why women choose to love somebody so they don't have to deal with nobody. Grasping at straws for which come first a pet, children, husband, or career has many living in turmoil. I want to encourage you to breathe. Stop worrying about what everyone else is doing, saying, and hoping for you. Take a minute to think about just you.

I know it is hard, and it was a harsh reality when I sat down on a therapist couch, and came home leveling with myself. My only regret with therapy is that I waited so long. As I write this chapter, I cannot help but think about the journey that brought me to this point. After experiencing four failed marriages, I finally recognized the common denominator in all these relationships. Me! My journey of self-discovery started during my second marriage. I began to notice familiar issues arising, and the relationship started to resemble my first marriage.

Have you noticed patterns about you? Do you have a type that you pick as your go to and are not sure as to why? Do you keep gravitating to life cycles that look like a repeat of a previous relationship with no avail? Are you tired of it yet? I identified similar patterns in the very early stages of the relationship before we married, even though I did not address them.

The issues did not disappear with marriage but followed us and only grew. It looked like I had carried my first husband into my second marriage, except he had a different face and name. If we are honest with ourselves during the dating phase, we will learn so much more about the person we are seeing and ourselves. When we hide the truth or run away from it, we hurt both parties involved. I saw that this life partner was controlling, manipulative, rude, and mean for no reason.

I didn't say enough about the treatment because I was just happy to be loved. I thought love was someone sticking around. I misunderstood honesty with name calling, nickpicking, and negative reinforcement as constructive criticism. I thought I needed to get stronger, but in reality it made me weaker. I felt helpless again about my life's position during my second marriage and as a result of this, I felt the need to pursue counseling.

It is okay to know you need counseling and get the help you need. It's okay to need a coach to help you get to that step or beyond. Our journey is ours and we own the results no matter which way they lead. If you need to go with someone, do that. If joining a group is the first step, I want to encourage you to do so.

I know there are matters that take time and dedication that go beyond social clubs or conversations with a friend. Initially, I attended couples counseling, but one of the therapists advised I needed individual therapy to address my issues. She emphasized for me to find solutions to my problems, I first had to have a clear understanding of myself.

I needed to understand my makeup. Who was I? What were my strengths, weaknesses, idiosyncrasies, and purpose in life? Why was I attracting the same type of partner? Knowing myself was crucial to breaking damaging life patterns.

I appreciate how my pastor emphasizes the value of introspection through the knapsack analogy. He says in every human's life there exists an invisible knapsack they carry on their backs. This knapsack represents the accumulated experiences, behaviors, emotions, and moods that are both positive and negative. He stresses the significance of regularly examining this knapsack and discarding unwanted items.

My pastor says some people carry knapsacks filled with dirty stinking socks while others have maggots crawling around inside. What a visual picture it was for me to see in my mind's eye. It made me think of what I was carrying and put a face on what I had tucked in my knapsack. It wasn't pretty, but some things had died inside, I thought maggots,(I jitter just thinking of it), were likely in there. These contents represent the negative thoughts, beliefs, and behaviors that no longer serve or contribute to my growth.

What thoughts, ideas, fears, and beliefs are you carrying in your bag? What is dead, stinky, or repulsive that you would instantly discard if you could see it, that you keep. Spraying perfume on funk or putting deodorant over dirt doesn't address the issue. We have to clean what is dirty and be okay with renewing to transform. Instead of taking the time to examine the contents of our knapsacks and getting rid of what is holding us back, we drag them around, adding to the weight of our burden.

My pastor believes the ability to take off the

knapsack and discard the things that no longer serve us is critical to personal growth and development. Without this self-reflection and introspection, we cannot hope to become better versions of ourselves. We will keep carrying the same knapsack, dragging it around wherever we go, and never being able to achieve true transformation.

Imagine carrying a heavy knapsack on your back wherever you go. It becomes a burden, weighing you down and impeding your progress. You continue hauling it around and allow it to grow heavier. Over time, the contents decay and start stinking. They begin to work against your evolution, but you keep hauling them wherever you go.

Sadly, many go to their graves with the knapsacks still strapped to their backs. They never take the time to reflect and grow or confront their inner demons; they can make the necessary changes to move forward. This chapter emphasizes the importance of doing the vital self-work to let go of the things holding us back and embrace the things that will help us become our best selves.

While it is crucial to seek support from others when we need it, we must take responsibility for our growth. The key to personal growth and healthy relationships is investing in ourselves. We must show up for ourselves. Failure to do so will keep us trapped in the same detrimental cycles. We will continue to experience the same struggles regardless of where we go or what we do. As someone said, "Wherever you go, there you are."

The importance of self-awareness cannot be overstated. Through personal experience and therapy, I have come to understand that having a deep understanding of oneself is crucial in making informed decisions about relationships. Through the journey of self-discovery, I came to understand those locked-away memories were the driving force behind my relationships as an adult. After a year of therapy, I started to uncover things from my childhood that had been holding me back in many areas of my life, mainly in relationships.

Through the journey of self-discovery, I came to understand those locked-away memories were the driving force behind my relationships as an adult.

Back then, I was unaware I had locked away those memories and thrown away the keys. I did not want to talk about them and certainly did not want anyone to know about them. It was sometimes painful, but I knew I needed to face my past to move forward. For a long time, I had buried those painful memories and refused to acknowledge them. But through therapy, I discovered that those experiences still affected me as an adult.

To be honest, some days I still reflect on my past but I don't allow what used to be shame to control my narrative. I don't allow the hurtful experiences to control the joy I crave. I wanted to pay it forward, so I started coaching other women on how to journey through this process like I did. It wasn't until counseling, I knew I needed a mentor and coach.

Going through the journey of counseling with no one to hold my hand at times made it hard. Sure, the process is hard, but I think of the many who would never sign up. Those that quit before the process is done. Most people attend counseling for a month and profess they are changed. It takes grit to keep at it for a year.

The road to self-discovery in that year was worth it and I want to help you by showing you what I learned. I realized that one of the main reasons I kept getting into relationships was because I craved love, acceptance, and validation at any cost. Additionally, I feared being alone and did not want to face societal stigmas that suggested I was not good enough to have a partner or keep a husband. Fueled by these emotions, I pursued and stayed in unhealthy relationships.

I realized one of the main reasons I kept getting into relationships was because I craved love, acceptance, and validation at any cost.

My therapist gave me assignments to work on at home, including meditation and self-reflection. I found it challenging to sit alone with my thoughts, but I knew it was necessary to truly understand myself. Through this process, I started to fall in love with myself. I did not need a relationship to validate me. I was enough...and more!

Self-work is essential for any relationship. Investing in ourselves is the key to breaking free from the cycles of failure that may hold us back. During this process of self discovery, I also realized how broken I was. I knew that as a broken person, I would only attract other broken individuals. I needed to become whole on my own before I could expect to find a healthy, fulfilling relationship.

So I did something I suggest you do as well, I started to date myself! I would dress up to the nines, treat myself to dinner and enjoy my company. It was a completely new experience for me. I had always been in a relationship. The idea of spending time alone was foreign, although I knew it was necessary if I wanted to heal and grow. I started doing things I had never done before, visiting new places, and truly learned to enjoy my company.

This process of getting to know yourself is ongoing, and even today, I learn new things about myself. But as I gained more knowledge and understanding, I began to set higher standards for myself and my relationships. I no longer allow myself to be a doormat or to settle for less than I deserve. Instead, I chose relationships based on my purpose in life and what I truly want.

If you were not taught certain life skills as a child, it can be challenging to navigate them in adulthood. You do not have a blueprint to guide you like others. You ask, "What chance do you have to succeed?" The answer lies in knowing yourself. This process includes researching and exploring ways to gain self knowledge. I had to spend time alone and learn to appreciate my own company. I realized that being alone is not bad and that self-knowledge is essential for any relationship, whether with friends or romantic partners.

I also had to stop blaming others for my problems and take responsibility for my actions. Other people can only reflect who we are on the inside. As a man thinketh, so is he. Additionally, I learned that love alone is not enough to sustain a relationship. To make things work, I had to truly understand myself, my needs, and take responsibility for my actions.

I also had to stop blaming others for my problems and take responsibility for my actions.

I have concluded that true wisdom does not necessarily come with age. It comes from applying the knowledge and understanding we gain about ourselves. Personally, welcoming God into my life played a crucial role in my journey. By letting God take the lead, I was able to gain a deeper understanding of myself, my purpose, and what I truly wanted in life. As a result, I was finally at peace with myself.

Thinking Points
1. Are you denying yourself of your wildest dreams because you stopped dreaming?
2. Do you put glass ceilings over what you can have because you believe they are not attainable?
3. If you could have any relationship you wanted, what kind of marital status would you want? Do you want children?
4. As a woman with a career and business, how do you feel your business has impacted your life?

Ambition is a great attribute but being overly ambitious can cause us to missout on the time to stop and smell the roses. For some of us, that means we miss the chance to spend time with our children or cultivate a relationship.

Exercise: I want you to survey your relationships and ask two questions: How is this relationship going? Is there anything I can do to improve this relationship? If you need help, I am here.

Chapter 5
Welcoming the Divine

Do you enjoy the rain or hearing the pricks of rain tap a glass window? If you don't have to run into a car to escape it, the rain is a welcomed calming sound. Is it not? Sometimes I find myself just sitting to hear rainfall or watch waves move in the sea. Nothing can be more relaxing than looking at water freely moving around.

We don't quickly see the force that gives water its power. We don't see currents, but can feel them when we are in the water. Similarly, we can feel the breeze and for the most part, we may not think of what is the source of its power.

Each and everyone of us are body, soul, and spirit, would you agree? If you believe in a Divine Source or not doesn't bear relevance as it pertains to it being real. If you feel the breeze you can relate to the wind although you may not know its source. In life, we live and breathe in air. We don't know the inner workings of our bodies to an infinite degree, but we can agree we exist.

In discussing, welcoming the divine, I acknowledge that some people do not believe in a higher power, and it is perfectly fine. I am not trying to preach to anyone; I am only sharing my personal experience of coming to terms with the presence of a higher force in my life and how that has helped me. I do believe embracing this element in your journey will bless you also. I believe the Supreme Being, God, orchestrates events in our lives for our benefit.

For instance, I ended up in the United States after winning the green card lottery, despite not applying for it. How can you win something you did not even sign up for? Unbeknown to me, a friend had submitted my name on my behalf, which is a story for another time. This experience taught me that if something is meant to happen in your life, it will. It is a reminder that God's ways are higher than ours and we should trust the journey even if it does not follow our expected course.

After my fourth divorce, I knew I needed a shift. I had tried and failed at love four times and did not know where to turn. Yes, I had 4 ceremonies, said "I do," got a ring, moved in, mingled families, all to end it. It doesn't take a rocket scientist to see that I had a problem I couldn't ignore. Do you have a rap sheet building up that points to a fundamental flaw in how you have relationships?

If you do there is no shame. I used to think of how embarrassed I was to say I had 1 marriage, then 2, I was super embarrassed to mention 3, and now to say 4 I feel as light as a feather! Who knew something so painful for me could be used to encourage others. I know people who shut their lives down after one divorce, but the Divine blessed me to be like the woman at the well. Yes I may have legally married my husband, but none of them were the husband I would keep.

Sometimes we do have to kiss and marry frogs to find our prince! I want to encourage you, your life isn't over after divorce no matter how many times you walk down the aisle. I had to understand what was my fundamental problem with marriage and accepting an attitude toward divorce. It was easy to do both and I got a double whammy on needing to make a change.

I got to a point where I couldn't point my finger at husband 1 and 2, not even 3 and 4. Something needed mending in me and starting my journey to love and date myself helped, but it was the tip of the iceberg. I had more work to do! I was on my way to getting whole, but if I wanted marriage, I had to accept that I wouldn't be single always.

Fear would make you think, if I get too comfortable I will not want to get married. Or, if I love myself too much, who could meet my standards or love me back? I battled many thoughts on my journey to 5 times the charm! It is likely you will too, but don't stop believing and pursuing what you want even on this journey.

I knew for sure that I needed guidance. If you repeat the same action four times and fail, you probably lack the necessary skills or knowledge to succeed in an area. That is the advice I would give anyone who finds themselves in a similar situation. If you have failed relationships one after the next, or if you struggle keeping a job, loving somebody, opening up about your feelings, it is a tell sign of a problem.

In the process of self-discovery, I began to question whether I was looking for love in the wrong places. Could it be that the love I was searching for in relationships was actually the love I wanted from God? It was then that I decided to welcome the Divine. After I exhausted every other option to find fulfillment, I reached beyond myself to welcome a real relationship with God. Not a Santa Clause version where He gives me what I want, but "The Creator" who tells me what I need, why I am here, and can change me.

In the process of self-discovery, I began to question whether I was looking for love in the wrong places.

There was no more ego-tripping. I acknowledged I lacked knowledge and understanding of certain aspects of my life and sought divine guidance. I invited God into my life and vacated the driver's seat. If you have been driving and crashing habitually, move out of the way. This doesn't mean you won't be in the car. Working with God to transform your life is a partnership. Charlene Harry has a beautiful message about how we are to Co-Create with God.

Instead of relying on my flawed judgment, I began to trust in the wisdom of the Divine. I let go of my fears and doubts and embraced the love and peace that comes with welcoming God into our lives. The jigsaw puzzle pieces of my life began to find their positions.

Gaining this new perspective allowed me to ask myself some critical questions. What exactly am I chasing in life? What am I looking for in a partner?

What is this longing in me that makes me think I have to be in a relationship to be happy?

Looking back at my childhood, all I yearned for was unconditional love for who I was, including my lef handedness. I desperately sought acceptance and love from anyone who would offer it to me, no matter the cost. When God entered my life I got a better understanding of what LOVE is. I learned God is love, and we were all created as co-creator. The Divine wants to have a relationship with us, and this born identity we all have, makes us desire relationships with others.

After my failed marriages, I realized all humans are flawed, and making mistakes is part of human nature. If I wanted someone to love me unconditionally, I needed to be willing to love them unconditionally as well. I learned the key to having successful relationships was starting them with a solid foundation. My relationship with God was my foundation and new example for how to have healthy relationships. God loves me unconditionally and I do not have to worry about anything. After all, most of what we accomplish in life is not solely the result of our efforts; they are divinely orchestrated.

I discovered that only God is perfect; we are all flawed. By establishing an intimate relationship with God. I no longer felt broken, empty, or the need to force myself into relationships, especially when there were red flags.When I came to that comfortable place where I allowed God to take care of me and what concerned me, I found peace and contentment. I was no longer worried about who was loving or not loving me. I no longer felt compelled to be in a relationship at all costs.

      Instead, I could just be myself and have faith everything would work out as God intended. If God is our anchor, we have a solid foundation. We no longer need to continue searching or scouting for that perfect love that does not exist among humans. Only when we allow ourselves to be led and controlled by God, can we find peace and contentment. If it is part of the plan we will have a partner to spend the rest of our lives with. This person will show up at the right time when we are in a relaxed and happy place.

> I was no longer worried about who was loving or not loving me. I no longer felt compelled to be in a relationship at all costs.

      I reached a point where I was happy with who I was, and as a result, I attracted happy things into my life. Our emotional state determines the nature of the things we attract: A happy disposition draws happy things, while a sad disposition invites only sorrowful things. I was no longer running around in a frenzy, anxious about who, when, or how. When I got to that point, the right person showed up.

> Our emotional state determines the nature of the things we attract: A happy disposition draws happy things, while a sad disposition invites only sorrowful things.

Now, I'm not saying that my life is perfect. I still face challenges and struggles, just like everyone else. But I know I am not alone. I have the love and support of God, and that knowledge gives me the strength to keep going. If you are in similar circumstances, I urge you to embrace the divine in your life. You may be amazed by how much a single action can improve your circumstances.

Thinking Points
1. In what areas of your life do you feel you have given it all you got, but the changes are not happening fast enough? Is it your health, within your marriage, on the job, or etc? List the areas and the problem(s).
2. Do you feel overwhelmed by the problems you are experiencing?
3. Are you worrying yourself daily, can't sleep, but you know you need divine intervention in this stage of your life?

4. Have you ever prayed before, sincerely prayed to get an answer to your problem or situation?

Oftentimes life can challenge what we believe. When we think we cannot take anymore, it is amazing how one more thing can be added and you are still standing. I want to challenge you, to lay your burdens down in prayer. I want you to accept that you are not a superhero, but a natural woman or man. You were born with talents and gifts, but also challenges and shortcomings.

Exercise: It is normal to not be perfect at everything. I want you to take inventory of the things bothering you right now. I want you to write them down. Next, I want you to repeat this simple prayer or affirmation, and feel free to write your own.

"I want to say thank you for the breath in my lungs and the ability to be here and make my petition known. Everything I wrote down on this paper had made me heavy but I am willing to let it go because You said your yoke is easy and your burden is light. I need to be made lighter at this moment. Please give me the strength to accept the things that will not change and the desire to change the things in my power. Today, I am lighter, I am hopeful, and I am professing my life is changed because I am embracing the Divine to help lead me in the right direction for my life. Thank you!"

Chapter 6
Practicing Detachment

Are you holding on to relationships for a false sense of security? Are you holding on to ideas about yourself that have you stuck in place? Do you see a pattern of you repeatedly using toxic relationships as your security blanket?

Recall how a toddler uses a security blanket. They keep it in their hands, they cry when it leaves, and they seem to have peace when they have it. The blanket can be dirty, old, tattered, and that love doesn't dwindle. They cannot enjoy other aspects of life, going to people's houses or being at functions without it. It is as if this blanket has engulfed and is at the center of anything important.

In our relationships, the only thing we should demand this much attention from is God. When we put this much energy, love, and longing in a person, we will drastically fall short of providing anything beyond the facade. The security blanket doesn't represent any true power, but it has a perceived importance that we give to it. The truth is, we can live without anyone and be able to enjoy life. Living with someone and loving someone is a choice. What we cannot live without is "LOVE" itself and that is "God".

Now, how can you shift away from people being your security blanket, to allowing God to use people to cover you? A covering as I have learned it in the context of God's plan is very different from the man-made version. God's version actually supplies safety, correction, and support. Men and women were not created to be alone, and we were intended to help and grow with each other.

A question that should be asked, How does something so pure become toxic? How does something sweet to your soul turn sour? When we put attention unorchestrated by God we have to unlearn, and detach ourselves from those things, ideas, and even people. In the Old Testament we see how God told people to detach themselves from people they married. We see how God says through Jesus He came to divide. He divides those who will follow His lead from those that will not in the context those who allow His plans to be higher, reach a different plateau.

There is an advantage to trusting in an all

knowing and powerful God. I want to show you how I practiced the concept of detachment. Then how it can help you achieve a greater sense of wholeness, purpose, fulfillment, and inner peace in life. Detachment is often misunderstood and often associated with a cold or indifferent attitude. Contrary to popular belief, it is a powerful tool for letting go of our attachment to specific outcomes and trusting in a higher power.

As we embrace something greater than our desires and needs, we experience peace and purpose. This new way of looking at life and situations has involved opening myself up to God and relinquishing my desire for control. Inviting God into my life has been essential to finding meaning and fulfillment.

As many have discovered, surrendering control to God profoundly impacts one's emotional state and overall well being. When I released the reins and allowed God to take charge, I experienced a sense of well-being, love, and joy that I never had before. I encountered an unconditional love that filled the void I had carried since childhood. I no longer needed external validation to feel fulfilled. I felt alive! The desire for a partner or relationship faded away. I realized my happiness no longer depended on specific outcomes or circumstances.

> I realized that my happiness no longer depended on specific outcomes or circumstances.

Whether it was a partner or any other desire, I learned to go with the flow and let God lead the way. By relinquishing control and allowing things to unfold naturally, I practiced detachment of outcomes. I trusted in the wisdom and guidance of the Almighty God. I had to realize I am not in control of anything, God is. My role is to discover and follow my path and purpose in life, which opens me up to all that is mine and is meant for me.

Our partners and relationships play a significant role in our purpose in life. However, it is important to remember they may not always come in the shape or form we are familiar with. We must be willing to go with the flow and trust in the divine plan. My partner is not someone the 'old' me would have selected, but he is the right one for the new me!

Maybe you will also learn in order for you to be ready for the right one, you have to dump the old. I have an unmarried friend who also does not have children, but her unwavering faith in God brings her inner peace. Despite the comments and questions from others about her biological clock ticking and the need to find a husband, she is unwavering in her faith. She believes God will give her a husband when the time is right. This unshakeable foundation in God allows her to face her current single season with grace and dignity.

When we feel secure in our beliefs and values, we are not easily swayed or fearful of any situation that comes our way. We can face life without fear or worry. Detachment of outcome can be applied to every aspect of life. I believe nothing happens by chance or mistake and that everything is part of a divine plan. If we permit God to guide us, we can fulfill our purpose and destiny in a state of composure.

I firmly believe every person is born into this world for a specific reason or purpose. It is essential to understand that when we let God take charge, it has to be in every aspect of our lives; emotions, finances, relationships, and all that pertains to life. We must trust that God has our best interest at heart and will guide us in the right direction. I am talking about practicing detachment of outcome in every situation, not just some. Letting go, and letting God.

Let me share an example from my life of practicing detachment. After going through four failed marriages, I finally admitted to not knowing how to choose a spouse and surrender to God. I had done the necessary self-work, learned to let go and let God. I focused on myself, my children, and my business only for a span of time. I started traveling and enjoying life.

Then out of the blue, someone I distantly acquainted with through a family member sent me a message saying "hello." At first, I thought maybe he needed a favor from me, but he proceeded to ask me if I was still single. I thought to myself, "Where is this question coming from?" When I said "yes," he asked me if he could introduce me to his friend, who was going through a divorce but was open to love again. I agreed, and he gave his friend my number, and we started talking. We continued talking for about a year.

Initially, I was hesitant because I was used to finding my partners. However, I realized when you are open to the Divine, you no longer have to control everything but make a choice to be open . Yes, I am sure you noticed every connection is not God ordained or meant to last forever; but some are! How many things have you missed–or would, if the 'old' you had been in charge?

I can tell you honestly, I would not have picked the guy I am dating for myself even with my new mindset because he did not fit the typical mold of a guy I used to date. When we begin the road to transformation, it does not mean everything about us has changed, but we do subject everything to change. We have to be willing to learn, re-learn, and unlearn.

Now, this does not mean there is anything wrong with him. On the contrary, there is a lot right with him. Sometimes, you just have to be open to change but that does not mean you have to compromise what you truly want and desire. God knows your heart! When I asked myself what made my partner stand apart, I concluded it was his heart. He has a heart of gold, and that makes all the difference. Everything else is simply icing on the cake!

If the 'old' me had been in charge, I would not have picked him because he did not fit the typical mold of a guy I would date.

As I have permitted God to work in and through me, I have experienced a sense of wholeness. By releasing my fixation on results and perfection, I have been able to focus on my life's purpose. Knowing that God is guiding me toward the correct path and everything will fall into place, I am at peace.

Let me end with a quote from one of my favorite authors, Tosha Silver:

"Oh Divine Order, all is perfect and happening according to a greater plan. The perfect solution to any problem is already selected, if you allow yourself to be guided. Divine Source says there is a natural, universal abundance that knows how to meet every need. Harmonizing with this force of love, call it the Shakti, call it God, call it Goddess, call it what you will, is the golden key to everything."

Thinking Points
1. Don't be afraid if the old you is uncomfortable with not being in control. It is normal, same as people rejecting your changed self.

2. Are you embracing the power of "no"? I want you to practice saying "no" to everything and person you need to for your healing.
3. Are there relationships that you realize at this juncture are not good for you and your healing process?
4. What can you do to detach yourself from the people or situations causing your downfall?

After reading most of this book, how are you feeling about the chapter's thinking points? Do you feel more sincere about being your authentic self? Are you more comfortable embracing who you are now than before?

Exercise: Write down your thoughts below. Also, what areas are you still struggling with? Honesty is the best policy for healing.

_____
_____
_____
_____
_____
_____
_____
_____
_____

Chapter 7
Living Your Best Life

Living your best life can mean different things to different people. For some, it may be achieving financial success, having fulfilling relationships, or pursuing their passions. For me, living my best life has been about handing over the reins to God in every aspect of my life. It has brought a level of contentment that I did not know was possible. Of course, this does not mean I have neglected my responsibilities or stopped putting effort toward my goals.

It is about finding a balance between doing my part and allowing God to guide me toward my purpose. Living my best life has been about permitting myself to be true to my identity, understanding my values, and making choices that align with my beliefs. This foundation has meant stepping out of my comfort zone, trying new things, and betting on myself.

My journey began as a left-handed child. The negative experiences resulting from being born with the trait shaped and influenced how I gave and received love in romantic and platonic relationships. As I have mentioned, through counseling, therapy, self-help, and life experiences, I have healed and evolved into the person I am today. I did not get here by myself and I continue to work on myself with the guidance of God and help from others. We were created to have friends and relationships so we do not live life alone.

This does not mean you have to get married if you don't want to, but we all need friends. We need people who will be there for us, encourage, support, and yes, also correct us with love. We all have room for growth and progress. The good Lord above did not create a world full of people to have us live in isolation.

Today, I can say that I am writing from my scars and not my wounds. I have grown in every aspect of my life. I attribute this growth to allowing God to take control and being honest with myself. When we allow God to guide us, things fall into place effortlessly. As long as I did what I wanted to do, directing my way, I found my end result was the same. No matter the face, these relationships ended the same, in divorce.

I can tell you that being on the other side, life becomes easy and seamless, when we make room for God to lead us. As I learned to detach from my old ways and embrace the new, my life changed. When I began to love myself, it opened me to receive love in the way I desired.

Positive thinking and living does make room for your life to get better. You do not have to struggle or fight to make things happen. When you are walking in your purpose, blessings and good things will come to you. Your main assignment is to be open.

Although I have gone through failed marriages, losing businesses, and money, I have no regrets about what I have been through. Don't regret your journey as it was a part of making who you are. Life is not always a bed of roses, and everyone experiences failures at some point.

> When we allow GOD to guide us, things fall into place effortlessly. Life becomes easy and seamless, and we do not have to struggle or fight to make things happen.

Worthy to note, with each challenge, I have become stronger and more resilient. Through these experiences, I have become a phenomenal woman. Growing up, I had to navigate difficult situations and circumstances that forced me to create my safety nets and build structures that supported and carried me through life. I am grateful for my life and am at peace with what I went through.

> Far too often, people get stuck in their past and allow the wounded child within them to continue running the show.

This journey has been a challenging one, but it has also been incredibly empowering. I trust as you have read this book you have been challenged. You see the growth you have made by hearing a part of my story and learning of my process. My heart's desire when writing this book was to share the valuable resources I have gained with you and others who have gone through similar experiences.

One area I am particularly passionate about is helping individuals journey back to their childhood and unpack how their past experiences are impacting their lives and relationships in adulthood. Far too often, people get stuck in their past and allow the wounded child within them to continue running the show. Ultimately, this leads to negative patterns and behaviors that impact their lives and relationships well into adulthood.

Through my own healing process, I have come to realize that it is possible to take back your power and break free from negative childhood cycles. I want to bring out the GIANT in you that I learned was within me. As adults, we have the ability to make conscious choices and create better outcomes for ourselves. By letting go of the traits and behaviors we developed to deal with childhood trauma, we can move forward and enjoy healthier relationships and a more fulfilling life.

I learned to embrace my power, uniqueness, and purpose. I wasn't sent to earth just to suffer. I know sometimes you probably feel like I did at one point, life equaled pain. I pray you allow me to show you life can be more than pain. We can experience love, hope, dreams fulfilled, and live a life worth living despite the pain.

Throughout this journey, forgiveness played a significant role. At some point, you must release those who caused you pain and harm to move forward and start the next chapter of your life. It is time to release those whose presence or the menting of their names makes your blood boil. These are the ones who really get you worked up. You must also let go of the strong grip they had on how you saw your past, including the hurt, trauma, and pain.

I had to repurpose my life experiences and take them from a painful truth to a resource that can help others. I share my story to help you and others. These experiences are not negative; they are part of the fabric of your journey. Without them, you would not be who you are today.

Although some of these experiences may

be difficult to revisit, you must eventually release them. It is my mission to help others recognize and harness this power. By sharing my story and the resources that have helped me on my journey, I hope to inspire and empower others to take control of their lives and create positive change. Together we can break free from the past and create a brighter, more fulfilling future. We have the ability to discard those coping mechanisms and behaviors that were once necessary for surviving childhood trauma but are no longer beneficial.

It is important to remember everyone's journey is unique, and the process of letting go and moving on can look different for each person. It may involve seeking support from friends, family, and therapists to find healthy ways of expressing and releasing emotions. The goal is to make peace with the past and embrace the present. I want you to look toward the future with hope and optimism.

Ultimately, living my best life has been about finding and loving me, flaws and all. Finally, I am living and loving authentically. I am free from the ball and chain of childhood trauma. I am beyond grateful for the present but am still striving toward a better future.

Thinking Points
1. How are you feeling about how you were uniquely made? Do you feel encouraged to be you or still feel a need to hide and ask per-

mission to be loved?
2. Are old habits creeping back into your progress journey or are you feeling more lost now than at the start of the book?
3. Have you embraced getting help from others that can assist you on this journey to healing?
4. If you can pull out 3 things you learned (or were reminded of) from this book and apply them to your life, what would they be?

Great job on finishing this book. You should be proud of yourself for your commitment to start and finish this book! We should not be so focused on the major accomplishments to the point we miss the smaller ones. All great test, small and large, should be acknowledge. It is the small things that make a big impact when full grown. Be patient with yourself as you travel down this journey. Lastly, I want you to take this last exercise and make it about you.

Exercise: I want you to write your story. What key elements have you lived through as a child? How have those experiences impacted your attitude about yourself? What good talents do you have and what are areas you are working to improve? Lastly, I want you to write out your own affirmation that will be your motto going into tomorrow, this week, or for the year. I want you to get comfortable thinking about your future, healing, and progress. Remember, to write it down and speak it aloud into the cosmos.

___

Let's Connect

We have spent so much time together it seems weird for us not to become friends because we do have a common bond that can help us grow to achieve our goals in life. If you don't mind, I invite you to join my Facebook Group: LeapingGIANTS and connect with me using my social handle: @KemiSpeaksOfficial on IG and Facebook. Also, please visit my site by scanning the QR code to learn more about my events, coaching programs, and future books.

Kemi Speaks

RECEIVE
"HEALING FROM EMOTIONAL TRAUMA, BREAKUPS, AND BETRAYAL"
with

Kemi Itayemi

Kemi's 12 week course is specifically designed to help individuals overcome the emotional pain and turmoil that often accompanies trauma, betrayal, and messy breakups. Through a combination of sharing life experiences and practical exercises, her program provides a safe and supportive environment for individuals to process their emotions, gain clarity and perspective, as well as develop the skills and tools necessary to move forward with resilience. Kemi's experience and compassion is dedicated to helping each participant achieve their personal goals and overcome their unique challenges. So if you're ready to take control of your emotional well-being and start living your best life, sign up for her 12 week course today

Register @ KemiSpeaks.com

About the Author

Kemi is a nationally-sought teacher, life coach, published author, and leading voice in breaking negative patterns stemming from early life experiences. Kemi grew up in Nigeria before relocating to the US as an adult. She is anAfrican American woman of the diaspora residing in Virginia with her children. She earned her master's degree in adult education (M.A.) from the University of the District of Columbia Washington D.C.

Professionally, Kemi has had the joy and privilege of working as an academic instructor with the US Department of Labor and a language arts teacher in the Maryland Public School System. During her long illustrious career as a teacher, Kemi has seen first-hand how various developmental and psychological concepts relate to the quality of our relationships. Looking back at her own personal experiences, she realized that childhood experiences quite commonly are the source of anxieties, self-sabotage, poor self-image, low esteem, and many other traits that damage adult relationships.

Kemi draws inspiration from the Psalmist's words in Psalm 124:7,

Our soul has escaped as a bird from the fowler's snare; the snare is broken, and we have escaped. Consequently, her coaching and speaking platform focuses on helping people unpack their childhood knapsacks, thereby breaking free from negative cycles that stop them from living their best lives. Kemi guides people struggling with diverse relationship issues to identify the root cause and overcome these offenses.

SCAN ME

It's time to start and finish **YOUR Story!**

KLE Publishing specializes in helping people become authors. In as little as 15 to 90 days, we can help you develop your book and publish to 39,000 outlets!

Ghostwrite, Edit, Format, Publish
We can help from
Start to Finish.

KLEPub.com Store

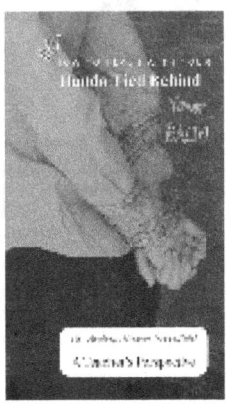

www.ingramcontent.com/pod-product-compliance
Lightning Source LLC
Chambersburg PA
CBHW052112110526
44592CB00013B/1575